Your Own Sky:
A Book of Breakups

Your Own Sky: A Book of Breakups
Copyright © 2026 BETH GYLYS
All rights reserved. No part of this publication may be reproduced or transmitted in any form or by any means without the prior written permission of the publisher, except for brief excerpts for the purpose of criticism and review.

For permissions and information on ordering books, contact operations@smallharborpublishing.com.

Cover art: Jennifer Wheelock, "Your Own Sky"
Cover design: Diana Baltag
Interior design: Brianna Chapman
Publisher: Allison Blevins
Executive Editor: Kristiane Weeks-Rogers
Managing Editor: Bianca Dagostino

YOUR OWN SKY: A BOOK OF BREAKUPS
BETH GYLYS
ISBN 978-1-957248-67-7
Harbor Editions,
an imprint of Small Harbor Publishing
Special thanks to: The Wild & Precious Life Series and Kristin Vandeventer

Your Own Sky:
A Book of Breakups

Beth Gylys

Harbor Editions

Small Harbor Publishing

For Tammy White, who has talked me through over 40 years worth of breakups.

Contents

Your Own Sky:
A Book of Breakups

Her mind lives tidily, apart
From cold and noise and pain,
And bolts the door against her heart,
Out wailing in the rain.
—from Dorothy Parker's "Interior"

Breakup As Revision with Lines by Yuri Andrukhovych and Dan Chiasson

I.
The wind is rinsing you,
and you stand there gaping.
Your mouth a voiceless chasm—
the loss of words blurring to a thin line
that knots into headache.

2.
The moon slides
through you
as you stretch on your back
across the living room hardwoods.
You are your own sky,
your own open darkness.

3.
Naked except for your mother's pearls,
you touch yourself,
try not to see his shadow
looming over you,
him pointing to your
dimpled inner thighs,
barely breasts.

4.
Your every lapse
is somehow his.
You grope for language—
puerile but also ancient—
he has stolen more
than you can name or remember.
Even standing, you're still
always on your knees.

5.
Hate is a terrible word,
like nuclear or penis.
It sits like a cinnamon ball
against the pouch of your cheek
where you tease it
with your tongue tip—
linger on the burn.

6.
Friends call, call,
knock. You will answer
one day soon. You will.
But now you need
this barren, this sand
sweeping the throughways
and hallways of you.

7.
*Worthwhile, worthless
what you loved,*
maybe forever you shift
one foot to the other like this.
You want to open
the box of it
and crawl inside.
You want to disappear.

***

Breakup as Revelation

That summer, stripped down to the raw, shell-less yolk of me—as if my skin had been pecked away by crows—I lumbered through the city past shrieking children flying high on swing sets, past bare-chested men jackhammering the street, past people cruising along on tides of busyness like vacationers riding jet skis.   You were in another state by then—you and the woman you'd one day marry. Block after block, I moved through the familiar unfamiliar, my present and future wiped clean as a window. I walked as if I was going somewhere, as if my steps could lead to better outcomes. In the end, and just as everyone told me, I surprised myself and didn't die.

My fat tears falling on the toes of your loafers, I once begged you not to leave me. Now I know I needed you to go years before you had the nerve.

Paradoxical Breakup Poem

Imagine, moving through the world as a set of teeth: *chomp-chomp!* That's what I'd become when I wasn't with him, starving for a drop of the salve of his voice, a shimmering glimpse as he turned down the hallway—the ghost of him sending a jolt, crown to crotch. I was crawling out of myself like a flea-bitten dog—everyone but him a cardboard cutout, every conversation (aside from the ones with him—his laughter opening rooms inside me) mere noise, the hum of tires along a nowhere highway. I had flown to a foreign country, and he was the only one who spoke my language, the only one who knew what to feed me, with his fingertips carelessly tossing small morsels in my direction. I lived there until I almost disappeared. Leaving was not an option. Leaving was the only option.

Inevitable Breakup

For more than a year we trudged
side-by-side toward the abyss,
barely speaking.

What was there to say? Both of us knew
the free fall was coming.

You routinely got drunk with your best friend.
I wept, touching myself in the shower.

We stepped aside in the kitchen like strangers,
our shoulders hunched from too much shrug.

In bed, exhausted with grief but fitful,
our bodies dog-eared Bibles gathering dust.

Who would we be as an I and an I
when for so long we had moved as one thing?

> *And the mind, amoeba-like,*
> *slips into empty*
>
> *spaces. The mind,*
> *steered by its own*
>
> *devices, made you*
> *if not enemy, alien.*

In therapy we read our lists of all we'd loved
then sat silent as stones in the rain.

You took my hand. At home, I leaned
against you as if to force myself back in.

We held on a little longer.
Then could not.

Love begins and ends
in gesture.

Breakup as Quadratic Equation

If *a* equals zero and *b* equals not zero, maybe we never meet on the stairs at your best friend's party, maybe the known value of us unwinds like a grandfather clock, our unbuttoned, unzipped clothes shimmying back on over torsos and hips, smoothing to pressed and pleated, erasing our coefficients. Does your value or mine make us nonlinear, our quotient appearing as fragments: your thin pacing wife, rays of light spearing my attic apartment, me in a bathrobe bent over double, you—gloomy and wordless—walking your dog? What would be the double root of our solution: hands shooing your marriage back into happiness or my real number the equivalent of someone else—a complex conjugate of no one like you? When c is no longer the possibility of we or us, what variables do we use to verify our results? How to define *x* that leads to the answer of nothing lost.

Nonstarter Breakup with Scrambled Eggs

We were finished before
we'd begun, our unfortunate
marriage of bodies; you lost
in my darkness and rocking sobs
folding me over you like a bent
playing card, the queen
of bad choices—you included—
your bewilderment almost sweet:
how you wrapped me in a towel
and pulled out a carton of eggs.

Eyes on the pan, you cracked
a smile that said, I am so done,
the eggs spitting grease, the sluice
drying on my right thigh;
no words, nothing but whisked eggs,
milk, cheddar, spinach, pepper, a dash
of salt—though the spigot in my brain
was turned on full—not even
a buttered slice of toast to make
this moment something more.

Magical Thinking Breakup Poem

When I found the wishbone, I knew it was a sign. I counted by sixes walking down stairs. I waited to see if you flinched when I brushed the hair from your forehead. I had to stir the soup eight swirls each time I opened the lid. When you FaceTimed your nun-sister, if she didn't mention the Virgin Mary at least once, if I didn't get to sit in row 23 on every flight, if I didn't see at least one blue jay a week… Avoiding cracked pavement, I walked around the block the same direction each day, veering a wide berth around the neighbor's black cat. Home, I'd drink water, two quick sips before setting the glass on the table. If you looked at me directly with one eyebrow raised slightly, I whispered an Our Father while crossing my fingers. If, when you closed the door, I heard the latch snap, I had to blink twice then take a low bow with my hands pressed against my heart. For years, I held us together like that, the shivering thread of us slender and fragile as a cobweb.

Breakup in the Form of a Prayer

Hallowed be thy early morning grunt, thy whiplash sneeze, thy six feet inches, thy snore, thy thick spread of butter, thy hacked up mucus, thy impatience, thy chinos, thy gulp of water, thy whole body laugh, thy loud telephone voice, thy slight pause, thy open-mouthed chew, thy distraction, thy mole on thy back, thy finger on my…,thy favorite ratty T-shirt, thy scowl, thy mother issues, thy warship nightmare, thy head slung back on thy pillow, thy sulk, thy perspiration stains, thy jock itch, thy wry smile, thy love of crows, thy anger at thy team, thy chase of a thief down the block, thy quiet, thy discouragement, thy lucky break, thy swallowed medicine, thy miscues, thy tongue on my…,thy middle finger, thy fear of heights, thy sore muscles, thy leg hair. *Forgive us this day.*

***

Breakup Questionnaire

1. Which of the following scenarios best describes your relationship?
   - a. We laughed, we cried, we landed in a bathtub filled with champagne and almost drowned.
   - b. I stood shivering in a forest, jackals peered from behind every tall fir.
   - c. He found her in a face plant on the tenth yard line. When she rolled over, the pin pricks of the stars disappeared.
   - d. *Hubba, hubba, hubba.*

2. Yes, no, or only sporadically, did you feel lonely in crowded rooms, Victrola playing in a corner, your lover in someone's lap?

3. Did you commonly wear any of the following to bed? (Choose all that apply.)
   - a. Spanx
   - b. A Chicago T-shirt
   - c. A coat of arms
   - d. A Rudy Giuliani mask

4. Which of the following options best describes your sex life?:
   - a. Squishy
   - b. We never left.
   - c. A dog suddenly stopped whimpering.
   - d. Stapled
   - e. In the key of D minor, the violins crescendoed.

5. When you think about your partner, what phrase or sentence best applies?

a. They smell of burnt leather.
b. MOM tattoo
c. Weak-kneed, I strap on the oxygen mask.
d. I stuffed myself with bratwurst.

6. In which of the following fantasies can you most imagine you and your partner featured?
   a. A town square. A mariachi band. Both of you in sombreros watching a goldendoodle chasing its tail.
   b. You're digging through a dumpster to pull out a stained armchair as your partner takes selfies with a juggling mime dressed in a polka-dotted clown suit.
   c. You wake up and you can't move. You hear the hum of killer bees.
   d. Looming over you as you shiver side-by-side and unclothed on a park bench, God takes a drag of his cigarette.

7. What famous RomCom movie line best describes the last time you felt close to your partner?
   a. "I like you, so there's that."
   b. "I'll have what she's having."
   c. "If you're a bird, I'm a bird."
   d. "I didn't think such violent things could happen to ordinary people."

8. What weapon from the following list is the one you would reach for in a duel with your partner?
   a. Unpeeled banana
   b. Heel of a red stiletto
   c. Playdough
   d. Hungry, feral cat

9. On a scale of 1–10, with one being least applicable or ten being most, rate the following statements as they speak to your relationship:
    a. Wrapped in bath sheets, we sneaked down a hallway past the unblinking eyes of tarantulas.
    b. You had me at corn dog.
    c. We didn't know whether to laugh or fall asleep.
    d. Tell me, tell me, tell me what you are!

Breakup as Naked Barbie on the Side of the Road

No, I said. One day I perched on the back of
his rented motorcycle, the next, I walked
through sun as if through a grove of
Ginsu knives. His curly blond
hair, his glasses, how funny/sweet
he had seemed, eating crawfish
beside me, the plastic red
checked tablecloth, the
black beads of their
eyes, the table
and floor of
strewn
shells,
loud Greek waiters shouting orders, a chaos
of crackers and long, skinny forks, Retsina
and Ouzo, and a walk on a long beach
beside ruins, the milky puddles of
the moon.   Was the doll a
Christmas gift? Did she once
wear a bathing suit? Bridal
gown? Gogo outfit? Did
she cheer? Own a cat?
A kitchen with a
mini stove,
fridge?
When does it change? A brother pulls
out her hair; the dog bites through
her neck, and there's always a
cute boy, more important
dressings-up. *Laughter.*
We were having
a good time,
weren't

we?
Lines from our feet blurred behind us
as waves devoured what was left of
the white coast. We went back to
my room. I was tired. He wanted
to stay. We did that dance.
He stayed. All the lines
blurred. All the
Nos.

Golden Shovel Breakup

after Gwendolyn Brooks

We called it a death, but
it was as much a birth, his
gone an opening, a flavor, like a mouth
discovering the taste of smoke. She would
become herself not
molded to an us, go
brow-deep into the thick of alone. Away
from the world, she bogged, mired, and
grew soft on beige foods. Neither
hungry nor satisfied, she would
eat, cry, binge-watch *Survivor*—the
irony, her meta rebellion—decapitated
future unspooling its ball of yarn. No exclamation…
more ellipsis, em-dash—no points
to aim toward, connect A to B—in
that open space, that
time of nothing next, she sank into other,
better, more: ample woman's
body—flint-sharp, fuck-all eyes.

Breakup as Epistemological Uncertainty

Inside that music, I knew who I was—intestines, snot, the knobs of my bones all suddenly making sense: the systems miraculously churning to make me me. I wasn't thinking about that though, was not even in my body really. I was not anywhere, which is far better than being somewhere sometimes. *Is this heaven?*, I might have asked. But I was singing off key and there but not there with the stained glass and the bloody Jesus looking despondent, his heavy dead body drooping on the cross (*his poor hands,* I said to myself)—Jesus bloody, floppy and frowning. No one in the whole place looked especially happy. *Maybe I am unhappiness*, I might have surmised. *Or sound. Or light— the way it moves through stained glass—maybe that's who I am: liminal and floaty.* I never have figured it out. The problem with God is the problem with air.

The Four-Legged Breakup

He was careless pretty the way that a boy
with long bangs and the look of wind sweeping
across a prairie can be. I mucked stalls
to keep him in alfalfa, rode hard his hard
back for so many hours my standing legs
formed a rhombus. I breathed dust and hauled
shit and wanted as only a teen girl
can want: a constant dull heat traveling
groin to throat, ever distracted by
the thought of him: his dark eyes shining
like river stones, his legs so muscular
and graceful that watching him walk, I knew
there was a God. When I left for college, I said,
I'm coming back for you. The kind of lie
we tell ourselves when we want to stay alive.

Fat Self: The Breakup That Wouldn't

She is all gnawing-the-sides-of-her cheeks, self-hatred gone rogue, so big she's stuck in doorways big. She sits on my face—butt an overstuffed sack of pillows, a set of netted cantaloupes, and I can't squeeze/squiggle/sidle out from under her. She drapes her arm across my shoulder, breathes her hot breath into my mouth. I want to say, *Now, go!*, like Gloria Gaynor, I want to *Avada Kedavra* her, but then I'm grabbing onto her like a buoy in a flood. We're hugging in a death clasp, drunken staggering around the room. I hold her so hard. When I look in the mirror, she's smiling in the way someone smiles when they know they have their index finger hooked so far up your left nostril you feel it in your brain. She's smiling in the way that says, *You're a sucker;* says, *I'll never let you go.*

Wish to Breakup With My Fool Head

Unfortunately, of late, never beset with bouquets or lined with pillows of fresh lasagna or lounging near some mango-splashed sunset, some gold pile of hay harvest. One day I woke with every direction the wrong way on a one-way. I should have been arrested. Instead, I didn't sleep for a week with all those bumpers rolling toward my bare knees. If you are like me, your pumpkin seeds all shaking in the pulp, you know what I mean. You too have awakened into a catastrophe of self, a circus of one, the trapeze flipped into knots, the brakes on your clown car metal on metal smoking.

Disproportionate Breakup Poem

She's giving off a TNT/nuclear fission vibe with her pursed lips and fuck-you face. She turns to walk away, and a bitter blast blows across you like the gust from an A/C unit turned on high. Your mouth stupidly agape, your open arms dropped to your sides after the snubbed hug, you stand confused in this one-way breakup, this dead-end alleyway of *no*: fat rats and murky puddles, the *drip drip drip* from the ledge of someone's window. You're too meager, too insignificant to her for so much drama. Behind the wall of her turned back you can almost hear the orchestra of machine beeps—a sheet draped across her son's thin legs, IV tubes hydra-like, his eyes sinking into silence. Her fury splashes like rain as she passes Moses-like through the crowd to get away. Whatever you have done—whatever you haven't done—will never be enough.

Breakup with Being Nice

A Visit to The Villages, Florida

I eat croissants all morning like a bored queen whose pastry chef is in love with her. Later, I will run through these landscaped-down-to-the-inch, indistinguishable, boxes-within-boxes tract homes—me jogging past, a wannabe assassin, cursing and aiming the pistol in my head at you and you and you: Fox News-gorging, gun-allegiant, golf-cart driving, anti-immigrant, anti-everyone-but-each-other, Christmas devotees. Today, I smite you and the red noses of your lawn Rudolfs, and your spoiled grandchildren with their SAT tutors and their perfectly straight teeth and their medals for showing up—you: book-banning, transphobic, other-disgusted, gay-is-a-choice-and-can-be-cured, MAGA cult-joiners moldering in your La-Z-boys. May all your toenails shrivel. May all your guns backfire. May all your grandchildren become as mediocre as their medals attest.

Breakup as Division

Inclined to stomp on red hats, to smack someone's bigoted grandmother upside the head, I try to think of her better qualities: she probably makes perfect homemade gnocchi, tucks in her grandkids with an Amen. The grout lines in her tub are likely as clean and white as a news anchor's teeth. What if we touched fingertips across the divide; what if we licked one another like cats with our rough tongues? Stripped naked we would shiver in front of each other, our fat rolls exposed, our bruises bright as pinwheels, half-moons dark under our eyes. Graffitied curses on our T-shirts, we ugly up even the clichés of our lives. I am out of ideas as the hummingbird moths circle the terrace unbothered, and from someone's window a trumpet's song stitches a patch into the sky.

Editorial Meeting, Phillips State Prison

The men are shy and rarely show their teeth. They sit with pens poised, nervous but also ready to say no. They tell us exactly what they think, not sure we will listen, though we always do. I don't tell them I hate violence, but I like the word slam: slam, slammer—not quite the same as smaller. Doors slam; hands slam on the desk. Here we speak softly as if telling secrets. Geese gather on the lawn. Their wings make us jealous. We speak, too aware of edges, too aware of how words can slip through keyholes. I have seen a word scale a fifty-foot barrier, scuttle down a drainpipe. There one goes now, ducking into a corner, about to springboard from the table to the fluorescent light fixture. Watch how it shimmies up the drywall and squeezes through the vent so fast you probably missed it. Words jump like fleas and are just as hard to squash. Let them get away, and they will never stop howling.

Dear Friends as Anti-Breakup

for Jennifer and Cathy

Every way you are threads through me like sap through
the branches of new trees, the green pulse of you
stretching and strengthening my arms and clavicles and
shin bones. When I wrap myself in the cloak you hand
me, I am no longer clown-like, wobbly on my unicycle. I
no longer impulsively pass out apologies like flyers to a
block party. Taller, steadier, the light's breath lingering on
the tops of the buildings in Rome like a peach wash, I
find something of myself that you slipped into my bag
when I wasn't looking. I finger it like luck, a faint smile
echoing on my lips that makes everyone wonder.

Breakup as Love Story

for Tom

Every day we spiral into our separate selves: flickering moths, so many lights fading into darkness, threads of thought like undone hems. If we touched fingers just so, you could hear a small sound on the moon. I could say, take me with you into the world, my love, and teach me who you are. Instead, the melon is so sweet, I suck each piece until the juice thrills my toes. Nothing you tell me is the same, which is only one reason to sing an aria. When you shower, I could envy the water's tongues on every surface of you. Later if we lie body to body, close as two sheets of paper in the thick of a ream, your breath is almost mine, rising like that, wave-like. And when I roll off you, if I listen carefully, the moon echoes back, a shiver like a ripe peach so thick with days of sunlight it has to fall.

Breakup as Revision with 1st Line by Judy Ireland

1.
I stand prayerless on your threshold.

2.
I stand on your threshold
choking, my mouth
stuffed with prayers.

3.
Every prayer the wind at my back—
you, my threshold.

4.
The prayers curses, a scream
blocks the threshold. Listen too long
and turn to stone.

5.
Too lonely to pray,
I curl at your threshold,
hands outstretched as if I might
gather air, make a thick braid
to climb down from the balcony.

6.
The threshold gone, I stand
in an emptiness, an archless
archway, you at dinner,
my prayers your crudité—
your plum gravy, your
raspberry millefeuille.

7.
Prayers like feathers
molting by your feet,
you smile at the threshold
still wielding the bloody dagger.

8.
Fragments of prayer—
a shredded, stained curtain
blown over the threshold.

9.
Sinks like a brick
thrown in a pond,
this prayer I think
far   from   any
threshold.

10.
We walk across
the threshold of each other,
prayers like moths
winging in our mouths.

Notes

The lines "*The wind is rinsing you…*" from Yuri Andrukhovych's poem "From 'Letters to Ukraine'" appeared in the March 2024 issue of *Poetry* and was translated by John Hennessy and Ostap Kin.

The lines "*Worthwhile, worthless…*" from Dan Chiasson's poem "*Euphrasy & Rue*" appeared in his collection *The Math Campers*.

The lines "*I stand prayerless…*" come from Judith Ireland's poem "Fireside Chat with the Goddess of Hearth and Home."

Acknowledgments

I am grateful to the editors of the journals where several of these poems have appeared or are forthcoming:

The Birmingham Poetry Review: "Breakup as Naked Barbie on the Side of the Road"
Nelle: "Dear Friends as Anti-Breakup," "Disproportionate Breakup Poem," "Fat Self: The Breakup That Wouldn't," "Magical Thinking Breakup Poem"
SWWIM: "Breakup as Revision With 1st Line by Judy Ireland" (under the title "Breakup as Revision")
Common Ground Review: "Golden Shovel Breakup"

Thanks to the staff and editors at Harbor Editions, particularly Beth Bolton and Kristiane Weeks-Rogers. You have been a dream to work with. To Cathy Carlisi, Jennifer Wheelock, and Ashley Grice for their friendship, love, and essential feedback and encouragement on early drafts of these poems. To Dustin Brookshire, who I adore and who gives me more credit than I deserve, and to Jennifer (again) for the gorgeous cover art. To Georgia State for ongoing support, and especially to my friend and department chair, LeeAnne Richardson, and her husband, Jim Diedrick, as well as my creative writing colleagues: Danielle Deulen, John Holman, Sheri Joseph, Heather Russel, Megan Sexton, and Josh Russell. To the students who inspire and teach me every day. Finally, thanks to my husband, Thomas Forsthoefel, on whose steadfast love I glide daily.

Award-winning author, Distinguished Professor at Georgia State University, and the co-founder/Principal Investigator of *Beyond Bars: A Journal of Literature and Art*, a Mellon Foundation sponsored literary journal for incarcerated writers and artists, Beth Gylys is the author of five books of poetry and three chapbooks. Her work has recently appeared in the *Birmingham Poetry Review, West Branch, The James Dickey Review, SWWIM* and on the *Best American Poetry* blog.

About Small Harbor Publishing

Small Harbor Publishing is a 501c3 nonprofit organization. Our goal is to publish unique and diverse voices. We are a feminist press, and we are committed to diversity and inclusion. We strive to bring new voices to a devoted and expanding readership.

Small Harbor Publishing began in 2018 with the first issue of *Harbor Review*. The magazine is an online space where poetry and art converse. *Harbor Review* quickly grew and now publishes reviews and runs multiple micro chapbook competitions, including the Washburn Prize and the Editor's Prize.

In July 2020, Small Harbor Publishing was officially incorporated and began Harbor Editions. Harbor Editions accepts submissions through a chapbook open reading period, a hybrid chapbook open reading period, the Marginalia Series, and the Laureate Prize.

In 2023, Harbor Anthologies began with a mission to promote texts that explore social justice issues and highlight marginalized writers.

If you would like to support Small Harbor Publishing, visit our "About" page at: smallharborpublishing.com/about.